WONDERS OF THE WORLD

Stonehenge

Catherine M. Petrini

KIDHAVEN PRESS

An imprint of Thomson Gale, a part of The Thomson Corporation

THOMSON

GALE

Detroit • New York • San Francisco • San Diego • New Haven, Conn.
Waterville, Maine • London • Munich

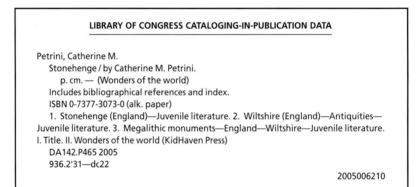

LIBRARY OF CONGRESS CATALOGING-IN-PUBLICATION DATA

Petrini, Catherine M.
   Stonehenge / by Catherine M. Petrini.
     p. cm. — (Wonders of the world)
   Includes bibliographical references and index.
   ISBN 0-7377-3073-0 (alk. paper)
    1. Stonehenge (England)—Juvenile literature. 2. Wiltshire (England)—Antiquities—Juvenile literature. 3. Megalithic monuments—England—Wiltshire—Juvenile literature.
I. Title. II. Wonders of the world (KidHaven Press)
   DA142.P465 2005
   936.2'31—dc22
                           2005006210

Printed in the United States of America

CONTENTS

A Mystery in Stone

On Salisbury Plain in southern England, a cluster of stones rises from a hillside. From a distance, it appears small, dwarfed by the vast, open landscape. Standing among the stones, however, most visitors are awed by their strangeness and sheer size. The tallest stand higher than a two-story house. Some of the stones are tall rectangular blocks called **sarcens.** These stand a few feet apart and are capped by slabs that rest across their tops. They look like doorways. Even the smallest stones—narrow, upright fingers of rock called bluestones—are taller than a tall man. This unique grouping of rocks is called Stonehenge. The name means "hanging stones," and it describes the way the horizontal slabs, or **lintels**, hang over the upright sarcens.

The main part of Stonehenge is a circular area. In its center, a large stone called the Altar Stone lies on the

Although there are many theories about its origins,
no one knows for sure why Stonehenge was built.

ground. Early researchers gave it this name because they thought Stonehenge was a temple. The stone's flat surface reminded them of an altar. Scientists have since learned that the stone used to stand upright and would have been too tall to be an altar.

Surrounding the Altar Stone are the remains of two arrangements of stones shaped like a horseshoe. The inner horseshoe once had nineteen bluestones, but only six remain upright. Others have fallen over or have been reduced to stumps. Some are missing altogether. The best-preserved part of Stonehenge is the outer horseshoe. It is about 45 feet (13.7 meters) across. It once consisted of five massive **trilithons** (meaning "three stones"). Each trilithon is made up of three sarcens. Two stand upright, with one placed on top to make a shape like a doorway. Today three of the trilithons still stand, along with a single upright stone from each of the other two. The stones of the sarcen horseshoe are the tallest in Stonehenge. The middle ones rise 24 feet (7.3 meters) above the ground. According to 18th-century researcher William Stukeley, their lintels were large enough "for a steady head and nimble feet to dance a minuet on."[1]

Outside the horseshoes are two stone circles. At one time, the first circle contained 30 to 40 bluestones. Six of them are still standing. Twenty-three others are either leaning, have fallen over, or are worn down to nubs. The sarcen circle around them measures 97 feet (29.5 meters) across. When this circle was intact, it had 30 upright sarcens. They rose as high as one-story houses and were connected by 30 curved lintels that lay across their tops to form a ring.

Outside the outer stone ring are several outlying stones and various holes dug into the earth. Some of the holes form circles. A large ring-shaped ditch surrounds almost all of Stonehenge, marking a space that is as far across as the length of a football field. Beyond the ditch are traces of the Avenue. This once broad boulevard curved from Stonehenge's outermost circle to the River Avon.

For thousands of years, Stonehenge has stood silently and mysteriously. It has inspired awe, serious scientific study, and some wild guesses about its origins. While its purpose is uncertain, its power and magnificence are clear.

Myths, Magic, and Mistakes

For hundreds of years, people wondered how normal people could have lifted the large and heavy stones of Stonehenge into place. They decided Stonehenge must have been built with the use of magic, or at least by more advanced people than those who lived in Britain in ancient times.

The earliest known writings about Stonehenge date from the 12th century A.D. The first reference appeared in a history of England written by Henry of Huntington around 1130. He described it as a place "where stones of wonderful size have been erected after the manner of doorways, so that doorway appears to have been raised upon doorway; and no one can conceive how such great stones have been raised aloft, or why they were built there."[2]

Merlin and Magic

A few years later, Geoffrey of Monmouth made up an entertaining story about Stonehenge's origins in his book, *History of the Kings of Britain*. His version of events centered on the wizard Merlin. By many popular accounts, Merlin was a friend and teacher to Arthur, a legendary British king of the 5th century A.D. In Geoffrey's "history," the stones came from Africa. Giants uprooted them from the earth and hauled them to Ireland. Merlin then used his magical powers to lift the enormous stones and carry them across the sea from Ireland to England. There, the wizard built Stonehenge as a monument to fallen British warriors. Geoffrey's story was

For centuries, people believed that the builders of Stonehenge used magic to put the enormous stones into place.

fantasy, but because he presented it as truth many people believed it. For hundreds of years Merlin's name was tied to Stonehenge.

Another history of Stonehenge was published around 1586. It appeared in *Britannia*, a popular but incorrect account of ancient British sites. Author William Camden claimed that giants had built Stonehenge. His only proof was that the rocks seemed too big and heavy for normal-size people to handle.

Romans and Druids

The 17th century brought some serious studies of Stonehenge. The first began when King James I of England hired an **architect,** Inigo Jones, to examine the site. Jones's survey resulted in the first book written entirely about Stonehenge. Jones and his assistant, James Webb, made detailed architectural drawings of the stones. Like many Stonehenge scholars, Jones believed the ancient **Britons** were too primitive to have designed and built the complex structure. Although Stonehenge does not look like **Roman** architecture, Jones concluded that the Romans, who invaded Britain in A.D. 43, must have built it. Another 17th-century researcher, Edmond Bolton, also dated Stonehenge to the time of the Romans. He suggested it was built as the tomb of Boudicca. She was a Briton warrior queen who led a revolt against the Romans. In fact, both Jones and Bolton were wrong. Stonehenge was built long before the Roman invasion.

Many 17th-century people thought the monument marked the location of buried treasure. Their reckless

Scholar John Aubrey thought that the ancient Druids who lived in Britain and France built Stonehenge as a temple.

digging turned up no coins or jewels. In fact, it may have disturbed key **archaeological** clues. One Stonehenge scholar of the time, John Aubrey, was different. His digging was cautious and well thought out. His goal was to understand the past rather than unearth treasure. As a result, he made several key discoveries. Most important, he discovered a ring of 56 holes just inside the bank and ditch that surround Stonehenge. These pits are called Aubrey Holes in his honor.

A woman standing next to a trilithon gives a clear idea of the tremendous size of the monument's upright stones.

Aubrey was a careful observer, but some of his conclusions were wrong. For instance, he suggested that the Druids (a religious group of priests, poets, and mystics) used Stonehenge as a temple. Before the Roman conquest, the Druids thrived in what is now Britain and northern France. Some people think they practiced human sacrifice. Part of the evidence given for Druids at Stonehenge was the discovery of reddish stains on one of the stones. Because the stains looked like bloodstains, it was called the Slaughter Stone and thought to be the site of Druid sacrifices. Modern scientists know that the stains on the Slaughter Stone are not blood. They were caused by rainwater reacting with iron in the rock. In fact, Stonehenge was abandoned a thousand years before the time of the ancient Druids.

Capturing the Sun

Aubrey's work influenced the next important researcher to study Stonehenge. William Stukeley was a doctor and clergyman. He drew accurate pictures and wrote detailed observations of Stonehenge from 1721 to 1724. He was the first person to identify the Avenue. Stukeley was also the first researcher to notice that some of the rocks of Stonehenge line up with the Sun's movement. This **alignment** can be seen on the summer **solstice** (the first day of summer, around June 21) and the winter solstice (the first day of winter, around December 21). These are the days of the year with the most and fewest hours of daylight.

Stukeley noticed that if he stood at the center of Stonehenge on the summer solstice, the Sun rose exactly alongside one of the outlying stones. This stone was a sarcen known as the Heel Stone. Originally the Heel Stone was part of a pair of sarcens. In ancient times the first sunrise of summer would have blossomed between the pair and shone down a stone corridor into the heart of Stonehenge. Six months later, sunset on the winter solstice would have been framed between the uprights of the massive center "doorway" of the sarcen horseshoe.

While Stukeley's archaeology was brilliant, his historical analysis was no better than Aubrey's was. Stukeley embraced Aubrey's ideas about Stonehenge as a center for Druid rituals, including human sacrifices. While Aubrey admitted that the Druid theory was only a guess, Stukeley presented it as fact. He even added to Aubrey's theory by making up and publicizing his own wild stories about secret Druid rituals at Stonehenge.

The designers of Stonehenge carefully placed the rocks to align with the movements of the Sun.

There are many unusual ideas about Stonehenge. As this illustration shows, some people believe it was built by aliens.

Science Fiction

Over the past 100 years, people have continued to invent stories about Stonehenge that they cannot prove. One popular group of theories links it to visitors from outer space. For example, some people believe space aliens built Stonehenge as a landing pad for spaceships. Another theory says local residents built Stonehenge after a visit from outer space. They designed it as a full-size model of an alien spaceship. Other people think the builders of the mythical lost city of Atlantis created Stonehenge.

For the most part, 19th- and 20th-century researchers used more scientific methods and have provided solid clues to Stonehenge's past.

CHAPTER TWO

The Rocks of Stonehenge

Modern science has revealed a wealth of information about the rocks of Stonehenge. Researchers now know what kinds of rock were used to build the monument, where the rock came from, and how it was prepared. Many guess at how the stones were carried to the site, but no direct evidence remains of the routes taken or the methods used.

The sarcen stones and bluestones are made of different kinds of rock. They came from different places and were brought to the site at different times. The bluestones arrived first, around 2550 or 2500 B.C. The stones are made of several kinds of **igneous** rock, or rock that is formed by volcanic activity. Although they look bluish when wet, the bluestones are really a blotchy brownish gray.

For centuries the source of the bluestones was unknown. The rock they are carved from does not occur naturally anywhere near Salisbury Plain. In 1923 a **geologist** named H.H. Thomas solved the mystery. He proved that the bluestones could have been quarried only in the Preseli Mountains in southwest Wales. This brought up an even more puzzling question. The Preseli Mountains lie 140 miles (226 kilometers) from Salisbury Plain. How did the bluestones get to England?

Massive Sheets of Ice

Some scientists believe that **glaciers** dropped the bluestones as they moved over the land. Glaciers are massive sheets of ice that once blanketed much of Earth. As

The bluestones of Stonehenge probably came from this quarry in the Preseli Mountains of Wales, 140 miles from the building site.

glaciers move over land, they often uproot rocks and carry them along. When the climate grew warmer several thousand years ago, glaciers in many parts of the world retreated to the north. Some Stonehenge researchers believe that a glacier once covered the monument site. When it moved northward, they suggest, it left the bluestones behind.

Other experts reject this explanation. They do not believe glaciers ever came as far south as Stonehenge. If glaciers had rolled over the landscape, the massive ice sheets would have left other rocks along the way as they retreated. There is no evidence of other rocks. Other signs of glaciers, such as marks left behind where ice scraped against rock, are also absent.

By Land and by Sea

Researchers still are not sure how the bluestones reached Salisbury Plain. Most, however, believe that people brought them there. Experts have identified two possible routes the people who brought the rocks from Wales would have traveled. Either way, the stones would have been carried partly over land and partly over water.

Along one route, people would have transported the stones mostly by sea. People would have moved them along the coastline of southern Wales and around the southwestern peninsula of England. Then they would have floated them up the River Avon. Finally, they would have hauled the rocks overland the short distance to the site, probably along the Avenue, which was built before the stones' arrival.

The other possible route involved more overland travel. After skirting the Welsh coast, the builders would have hauled the stones across the English peninsula instead of around it, making use of rivers when possible. This second route is much shorter than the water route, but it also would have been more difficult and dangerous. People would have had to lug the heavy stones up and down hills. Because of that, researchers think the water route is the more likely route the people traveled with the stones.

Each bluestone weighs about 4 tons (3.63 metric tons), as much as two sport-utility vehicles. To float the stones over water, Stonehenge's builders probably lashed each one to a specially designed canoe or raft. In recent times, groups of volunteers have re-created such journeys to prove that this method could have worked.

The fact that the bluestones came from so far away raises another question: Why did the builders bother to

A woman stands between 2 of Stonehenge's 80 bluestones. How the builders transported the bluestones to the monument's site remains a mystery.

Bluestones

This is a close-up of a bluestone, which may have had special meaning for the builders of Stonehenge.

transport them? Geologically, there is nothing special about the Preseli Mountain stones. Yet someone chose to transport them all the way from Wales, despite the time and difficulty. Nobody knows for sure, but some researchers think these bluestones had a deeper meaning to the people who built Stonehenge. Perhaps the stones were part of an older monument, a sacred place that is now long forgotten.

Moving the Sarcen Stones

Even more striking than the bluestones are the much larger sarcen stones, which dominate the monument. The sarcens are enormous slabs of a very hard kind of sandstone. People did not travel far to bring the sacren stones to Salisbury Plain, as they did with the bluestones. The stones were taken from Marlborough

Downs, hills located about 20 miles (32 kilometers) north of the Stonehenge site.

That distance is much shorter than the trek that brought the bluestones from Wales. The massive size of the sarcens and the uneven terrain, however, would have made this journey even more difficult. The heaviest sarcen weighs 45 tons (40.82 metric tons), as much as three large school buses. There were more than 75 sarcens to transport. Stonehenge's builders had to move the huge stones without cranes and other advanced equipment. In fact, their society probably did not even have wheels. Modern scientists can only guess at how this journey was accomplished. Some experts think the builders pushed the sarcens along on rollers made of large tree trunks. Others think they used heavy wooden sleds to carry the sarcens across the landscape.

The Heel Stone is a large, upright sarcen made of a type of sandstone brought from Marlborough Downs, 20 miles from the Stonehenge site.

Bluestone and Sarcen Stone Routes

Legend:
- Possible bluestone route
- Alternative bluestone route
- Sarcen stone route

SCOTLAND

North Sea

Liverpool

ENGLAND

Preseli Mountains
(140 miles from Stonehenge)

Marlborough Downs
(20 miles from Stonehenge)

WALES

London

Irish Sea

Stonehenge

Plymouth

River Avon

English Channel

Dressing the Stones

After they arrived on Salisbury Plain, both types of rock would have been dressed (carved into the desired shape), smoothed, and prepared for building. The carvers chipped away at the rocks with tools made of stone. The bluestones of the inner horseshoe were carefully carved into smooth, even pillars. Others, such as those in the bluestone circle, were left in a more natural state.

Shaping the sarcens was more complicated. Workers had to chip away at them little by little to form the squared-off shapes needed for the monument. Once a sarcen's basic size and shape were right, its surface had to be smoothed slowly and carefully. The sarcens are made of sandstone that is unusually hard. Even with modern tools, the rock is difficult to chip. Stonehenge's builders used primitive hand tools. Their tools, called **hammerstones**, were lumpy balls made of sarcen stone. It was the only kind of rock tough enough for the job. The largest hammerstones found at the site are as big as soccer balls. With them, workers could have pounded away at the sarcens to whack off large amounts of extra stone. The smallest hammerstones were the size of tennis balls. With these smaller, lighter tools, carvers could have gently rubbed or pecked at the sarcens to smooth their surfaces.

When the stones were shaped and smooth, early Britons would use them as building blocks to create Stonehenge. Stonehenge was more than a ring of stones, however. The monument was there in other forms, long before the bluestones and sarcens were carried to the site.

CHAPTER THREE

Building a Puzzle, Piece by Piece

One of the most important recent discoveries about Stonehenge is that it took different forms over the fifteen centuries that it was in use. These different forms are usually described in terms of three phases.

Earthworks

Phase One was an earthwork monument, also called a **henge.** Most experts think it began around 3000 B.C., or 50 centuries ago. In this phase, there were no stones at Stonehenge. Seen from overhead, the site would have looked like a large circular area surrounded by several rings. The outer ring was a narrow, low bank of earth. Just inside that bank, a ring-shaped ditch was dug into the ground. Inside the ditch was another circular ring of banked earth. This inner bank was about 6 feet (1.83

meters) high. Inside that bank was a series of 56 round holes, also arranged in a circle. These are the Aubrey Holes. Some people guess they once held wooden posts, but scientists are not sure.

The Phase One monument had two entrances. The main entrance faced northeast. It pointed to the summer solstice sunrise. The other entrance faced south.

Animal bones have been found at the bottom of the ditch, especially near the entrances. They include the jawbones of cattle, at least one ox skull, pieces of deer antler,

An aerial view of Stonehenge shows the ditch and Aubrey Holes, created before any stones were put in place.

and other fragments. Scientists believe they were placed there when the ditch was first dug. Some of the bones, including the deer antlers, are the same age as the ditch and were almost certainly used as digging tools for building Phase One. Some of the other bones are 300 years older than the ditch and banks. Scientists think they may have been religious objects kept for use in important rituals.

The Timber Monument

Phase Two was a **timber** monument, possibly in use between 2900 and about 2400 B.C. During this phase, a wooden structure was built in the center of the circle. In fact, the design of the wooden structure may have been copied in the stone monument that eventually replaced it. The structure consisted of upright wooden posts set into the ground in a complex pattern. It may have had a roof. There is even evidence of wooden walls that formed a narrow entrance. The rising Sun would have shone through this entrance on the morning of the summer solstice.

Builders of Phase Two seem to have deliberately blocked some parts of the ditch. The Aubrey Holes were also partly filled. Animal bones and the remains from human **cremations** have been found in the ditch and in some of the Aubrey Holes. These remains date from Phase Two.

The Avenue was also constructed during Phase Two. This was a 40-foot (12.19-meter)-wide roadway outlined by parallel banks and ditches. It began at the monument's northeast entrance and swung around to the right to reach the River Avon. It was probably used for formal processions to the monument for rituals.

Stonehenge as viewed from above, showing the bluestones and sarcens that were erected during the final phase of construction.

The Stones Arrive

Phase Three began with the arrival of the bluestones and lasted a thousand years. During this time, these stones were arranged in several different ways. The bluestones were the first stones to be set in place within the henge. These first bluestones were left rough. They did not have the smooth surface treatment seen later. The builders arranged at least 82 of them in two circles or arcs, one inside the other. This first stone monument was short lived. It was dismantled within a century.

Next came another portion of Phase Three. This was the placement of the sarcen stones. Unlike the bluestones, the sarcens were set once and never moved. Near the center of the site, workers built the five massive "doorways," or trilithons, that made up the sarcen horseshoe. Around this horseshoe was a larger circle of sarcens. These stones were topped by sarcen lintels. The lintels were curved and fitted together tightly to form a continuous ring of stone. Their design was so sophisticated that the lintel ring lay almost perfectly horizontal, even though the ground under the monument slopes. Such an engineering feat would be difficult even with modern construction knowledge and equipment. The fact that it was accomplished more than 4,000 years ago is remarkable.

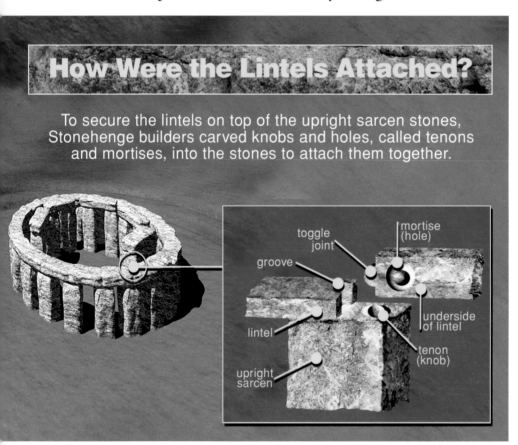

How Were the Lintels Attached?

To secure the lintels on top of the upright sarcen stones, Stonehenge builders carved knobs and holes, called tenons and mortises, into the stones to attach them together.

toggle joint

groove

mortise (hole)

lintel

underside of lintel

upright sarcen

tenon (knob)

Rather than just resting across the standing stones, the lintels are actually attached to them. This was done with **mortise-and-tenon** joints. On the underside of the lintels, workers gouged mortises, or holes. On the top surfaces of the uprights, they carved tenons, or knobs, sized to fit those holes. When the lintels were fitted over the uprights, the holes cupped the knobs, securely holding the stones together.

After the sarcens were in place, carvers decorated some of them. In 1953, Richard Atkinson was the first scientist to identify carvings on the surface of one of the trilithon uprights. He made out the shape of a dagger, about 1 foot (30 centimeters) long. Near it were more carvings, shaped like ancient axes. Because the carvings are so old, their outlines are very faint and easy to miss. Since Atkinson's discovery, scientists have identified carvings on twelve of the sarcen stones. Many are pictures of axes like those noted by Atkinson. The most mysterious carving is harder to identify. Some researchers believe it is a picture of an Earth goddess like those that have been found in ancient monuments in Brittany, a region in France. Others think the "goddess" is just a bumpy place on the rock.

Phase Three Evolves

After the sarcens were finished, the builders returned the bluestones to the monument. Evidence hints that they may have first set them in an arrangement that has been long forgotten. Eventually they moved them again. This time they arranged them into two groupings. Inside the sarcen horseshoe, more than twenty

Stonehenge Construction Stages

The construction of Stonehenge took over fifteen centuries and is usually described in three phases.

 In Phase I, there were no stones at Stonehenge.

 In Phase II, a wooden structure was built in the center of the circle.

In Phase III, the wooden structure was copied in stone.

Phase III lasted a thousand years. Stonehenge was abandoned in 1600 B.C.

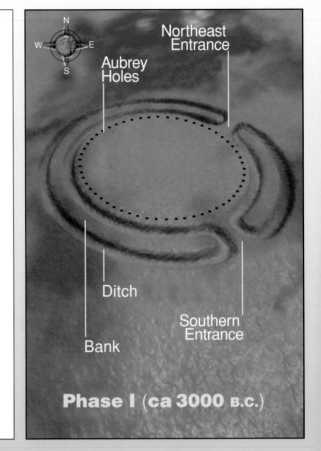

Northeast Entrance

Aubrey Holes

Ditch

Bank

Southern Entrance

Phase I (ca 3000 B.C.)

shaped and smoothed bluestones formed an oval. A circle of rougher bluestones was placed inside the outer sarcen circle. During this period, the builders may also have set the Altar Stone into its current position.

By around 1900 B.C., Stonehenge was almost finished. At this point, the oval of bluestones was rearranged to form a horseshoe. In the final portion of Phase Three, two rings of pits called Y Holes and Z Holes were dug, one inside the other. They were outside of the stone circles but well within the ditch-and-bank enclosure. The pits are rectangular. Many experts

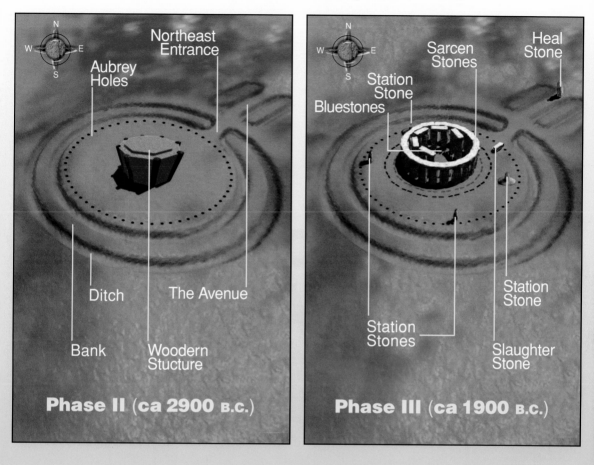

Phase II (ca 2900 B.C.)

Phase III (ca 1900 B.C.)

believe they were dug to hold more uprights. If so, those stones were never placed.

Stonehenge also includes six outer stones, which are all sarcens. The Slaughter Stone and four Station Stones are inside the ditch-and-bank enclosure. The Heel Stone is outside the enclosure, in the entrance to the Avenue. Scientists do not know when these six stones were placed.

After more than 1,500 years of activity on the site, Stonehenge was apparently abandoned around 1600 B.C. Scientists do not know why. This question is only one of the many mysteries of Stonehenge yet to be solved.

CHAPTER FOUR

Astronomy and Awe

To many people, the most tantalizing mystery surrounding Stonehenge is the most basic one: What was it used for? The site clearly had different uses over its long active period. Experts know that it was once used as a burial ground, but that is all they know for sure. Some believe that it could have been used as a calendar, an astronomical observatory, or a setting for religious rituals.

Tracking the Skies

Spaceship theories aside, it seems clear that Stonehenge's creators were thinking about the skies when they built the monument. The first evidence of this was Stukeley's discovery of the stones' alignment with the Sun at the summer and winter solstices. The Sun is not the only object in the sky that has been connected with Stonehenge, however. Twentieth-century researchers discovered that other features of the monument line up with movements of the Moon.

The first researcher to discover lunar alignments at Stonehenge was amateur astronomer Peter Newham, in 1963. He did not have the background and scientific equipment to complete in-depth studies, but his work inspired an American astronomer, Gerald Hawkins. Hawkins examined the relationship between the Moon's cycle and the four Station Stones. The Station Stones lie within the henge but outside the stone circle. Their positions can be seen as the corners of a large rectangle. The Moon rises and sets at different points on the horizon, following an 18.6-year cycle. Hawkins found that

Giant bubbles float through the air as a crowd at Stonehenge greets the rising Sun during the 2003 summer solstice.

the longer sides of that rectangle point to the spots on the horizon where the Moon rises and sets at the start and end of its cycle.

Hawkins and other researchers have also claimed that the Aubrey Holes were dug to predict lunar eclipses, but most experts reject this. Other studies have tried to find a relationship between Stonehenge and the movements of the stars. So far the evidence has not been convincing.

Still, the monument does seem to have been designed to track the movements of the Sun and Moon. This may have been done for practical or spiritual reasons. Most likely it was a combination of both. Keeping track of the seasons must have been crucial to the people who built Stonehenge. They lived in a society based

This image shows the four phases of the Moon appearing at different points over Stonehenge.

on farming, and farmers must know when to plant and harvest crops and when to expect certain kinds of weather. Their society had no written language. Without clocks or calendars, they probably tracked the seasons by watching the sky. A monument like Stonehenge could have shown them the exact time of year. Stukeley was the first modern researcher to realize this. Today most people believe this was a likely reason for Stonehenge's alignments with the skies.

At the same time, most believe it was probably not the only reason. Many ancient societies thought of the Sun and Moon as sacred. Modern experts do not know much about the societies that built Stonehenge. It is likely, however, that the Sun and Moon played a part in their spiritual beliefs, too. If so, Stonehenge must have been an important center for religious rituals.

Buried Bodies

Fragments of burnt human bones found on the site support the idea of Stonehenge as the site of religious rituals. During Phase Two, the monument was used as a cemetery for cremated remains. Many of the remains found there were those of children and young women. Some people believe they were killed as human sacrifices in religious ceremonies. There is no clear evidence to support this theory. More likely, they died of other causes but were buried at Stonehenge for religious reasons.

The exact spot where the remains were found may be significant. It lines up with the position on the horizon where the Moon rises at the southernmost point in its cycle. The fact that cremated remains were buried

This nineteenth-century painting imagines hundreds of ancient Britons participating in a religious ceremony at Stonehenge.

there suggests that the alignment was important to early Britons, but modern experts do not know why. "I think it very plausible . . . that there was perhaps lunar symbolism. The problem is the specifics,"[3] says Clive Ruggles, a scientist at the University of Leicester. Uncovering those specifics without any solid clues is nearly impossible. Instead researchers make educated guesses by looking at other ancient cultures. In many cultures the Moon symbolized death and rebirth. If the people who built Stonehenge thought about the Moon in that way, they might have used that symbolism in their burial practices.

In addition to the cremated remains, two human skeletons have been found buried at Stonehenge. Modern scientific analysis suggests that both men were murdered. One of the bodies was unearthed in 1978 near the Avenue. It was a young man who died about 2310 B.C. At 5 feet, 10 inches (177 centimeters), he was taller than other people of southern England at that time. This indicates he was probably not from the area. One clue to his identity is a slate wrist guard found on his arm. Such wrist guards were worn by archers. Flint arrowheads were found in his ribs, proving that he was shot by arrows. Nobody knows who shot him or why. Some scientists guess that he was sacrificed in a religious ritual meant to dedicate the new Avenue, but there is no direct evidence of that.

The other body was found in 1923, but detailed studies were not done until the 1990s. This was also the skeleton

A scientist holds the skull of a skeleton excavated from Stonehenge, perhaps the victim of ritual sacrifice.

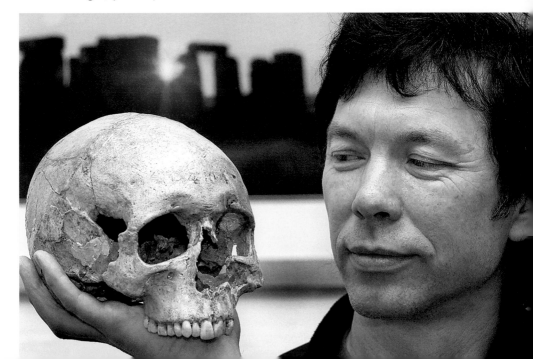

Modern-day Druids take part in a ceremony at Stonehenge. Today, the monument's mysteries inspire many different kinds of people.

of a young man, probably in his 30s. Analysis of the minerals in his teeth suggests he was a local resident. This man was killed by a sword that sliced through his spinal cord. He was buried in a narrow, shallow grave outside the stone circles but inside the henge. The body has been dated to the 7th century A.D., much later than the monument itself. That means the executed man had nothing to do with the society that built Stonehenge. Still, the find is important. It reveals that even when the site was no longer in regular use, Stonehenge was not completely forgotten. Later societies continued to find uses for it.

"Every Kind of Theory"

Today interest in Stonehenge has rebounded. Artists and writers still find inspiration in it. Modern-day mystics hold ceremonies there, as if it really was once a Druid temple. Scientists and historians still study it, trying to uncover new clues to its construction and early uses. Sightseers stand in awe on Salisbury Plain, gazing up at the mysterious stones and wondering about the distant past.

Writer William Long described the ongoing interest in Stonehenge's origins: "Every kind of theory has been proposed and so regularly combated. And so it will be till the end of time."[4] He wrote that in 1876, but his words still hold true today. While many of the monument's puzzles have been solved, the largest one remains. Five thousand years after its beginnings, nobody knows for sure what Stonehenge is or why it was built.

Notes

Introduction: A Mystery in Stone
1. William Stukeley, *Stonehenge: A Temple Restor'd to the British Druids*. New York: Garland, 1984, p. 35.

Chapter One: Myths, Magic, and Mistakes
2. Quoted in David Souden, *Stonehenge Revealed*. New York: Facts On File, 1997, p. 140.

Chapter Four: Astronomy and Awe
3. Quoted in Jean-Claude Bragard, producer and director, *Stonehenge*. BBC Manchester, 1998.
4. Quoted in Peter Lancaster Brown, *Megaliths, Myths, and Men: An Introduction to Astro-Archaeology*. Mineola, NY: Dover, 1976, p. 59.

Glossary

alignment: The positioning of objects in relation to other objects.

archaeological: Related to archaeology, which is the discovery and study of artifacts and sites left from past cultures.

architect: A person who designs and supervises the construction of buildings. The art and science of designing buildings is called architecture.

Britons: People who lived in ancient times in what is now Great Britain.

cremations: The burnings of human bodies after death.

geologist: A person who studies Earth's structure.

glaciers: Huge masses of ice that survive from year to year instead of melting away. Glaciers can move across the land.

hammerstones: Pieces of rock shaped into balls to be used as tools for pounding. Also called mauls.

henge: An ancient site made up of a circular area surrounded by a bank and a ditch. Originally, the word meant "hanging."

igneous: Formed by volcanic activity.

lintels: Beams placed across the top of two uprights to create a structure like a doorway.

mortise-and-tenon: A building method that connects two pieces of material by fitting knobs (tenons) on one piece into holes or sockets (mortises) in the other.

Roman: Having to do with Rome, now the capital of Italy. Between 27 B.C. and A.D. 410, Rome was the center of the largest, most powerful empire on Earth.

sarcens: The largest stones at Stonehenge. They are made of very hard sandstone.

solstice: The first day of either winter or summer. In the northern half of the world, the summer solstice is around June 21 and has the most hours of daylight of any day of the year. The winter solstice is around December 21 and has the fewest hours of daylight of any day of the year.

timber: A large, square piece of wood used to form structures.

trilithons: Prehistoric structures made by placing one stone horizontally across the tops of two upright stones. Literally the word means "three stones."

For Further Exploration

Books

Rachel Lynette, *Stonehenge*. San Diego: KidHaven Press, 2005. Part of the Great Structures in History series, this book explores the construction, history, and mystery of Stonehenge.

Nancy Lyon, *The Mystery of Stonehenge*. New York: Raintree, 1977. In this practical, highly readable guide to Stonehenge studies, Lyon covers theory, history, terminology, and fascinating facts. Written in clear, everyday English, with an occasional touch of humor.

Caroline Malone and Nancy Stone Bernard, *Stonehenge*. New York: Oxford, 2002. This overview highlights early theories about Stonehenge, the people who built it, and likely ways the stones could have been brought to the site and set into place. It includes a glossary, time line, bibliography, and colorful maps and illustrations.

Video/DVD

Jean-Claude Bragard, *Stonehenge*. BBC, 1998. This production, made in conjunction with The Learning Channel and Time-Life, traces the origins and meaning of Stonehenge and speculates about rituals that might have taken place there. In particular, the film explores Stonehenge by comparing it to other ancient monuments in England and around the world.

Matt Ford, *Stonehenge: A Journey Back in Time.* Cromwell Films, 1998. Part of the series *Lost Treasures of the Ancient World*, this film uses computer animation to re-create Stonehenge in all its phases.

Jeremy Freeston, *Murder at Stonehenge.* Educational Broadcasting, 2001. This entry in the popular PBS series *Secrets of the Dead*, is like a prehistoric police drama. It traces the detective-like work done by Mike Pitts, the young archaeologist who analyzed ancient forensic evidence to learn the truth about a skeleton unearthed at the site. Includes historical background on Stonehenge as well as a fascinating look at the science of archaeology.

Kelly McPherson, *The Enduring Mystery of Stonehenge.* A&E Television, 1998. Part of the History Channel's *In Search of History* series, this film focuses on the more puzzling aspects of the monument, including some controversial theories. Stonehenge experts discuss the mystical significance of the Sun and Moon, human remains found at the monument, and methods that may have been used to transport the stones to the site.

Web Sites

About Stonehenge (www.aboutstonehenge.info). This Web site aims to be the one-stop spot for all things Stonehenge. It includes history and legends, data on astronomical alignments, tourist information, and Stonehenge-related educational activities such as a "Build Your Own Henge" game.

English Heritage (www.english-heritage.org.uk). This is the official site of the agency that runs Stonehenge. At the top of the home page, click on the large photograph of Stonehenge. The site includes historical background as well as visitor information, photographs, and plans for Stonehenge's future.

Secrets of Lost Empires: Stonehenge (www.pbs.org/wgbh/nova/stonehenge). This is the site for the *Nova* miniseries that aired on PBS. The "Secrets" programs attempted to reconstruct technological feats from the past. In the Stonehenge episode, volunteers transported concrete blocks the size of sarcens from Marlborough Downs to Salisbury Plain and then built trilithons, using only tools that were available in prehistoric times. Behind-the-scenes facts are revealed in the transcript of an interview with an archaeologist who worked on the series.

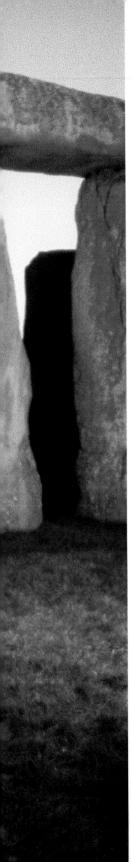

Index

Picture Credits

About the Author

Catherine M. Petrini has written 27 previous books. They include everything from a novel about a werewolf to a nonfiction book, *The Petronas Towers* (Blackbirch Press), on Malaysia's record-breaking skyscrapers. Her twenty young-adult novels were written under pseudonyms for the Sweet Valley High series and other teen series. Recent nonfiction books include *The Italian Americans* (Lucent) and *What Makes Me a Muslim?* (KidHaven).

Petrini, a former magazine editor, is a frequent speaker on writing-related topics and hosts a radio show. She has a bachelor's degree in English from the University of Virginia and a master's in writing from Johns Hopkins University.